AF573771

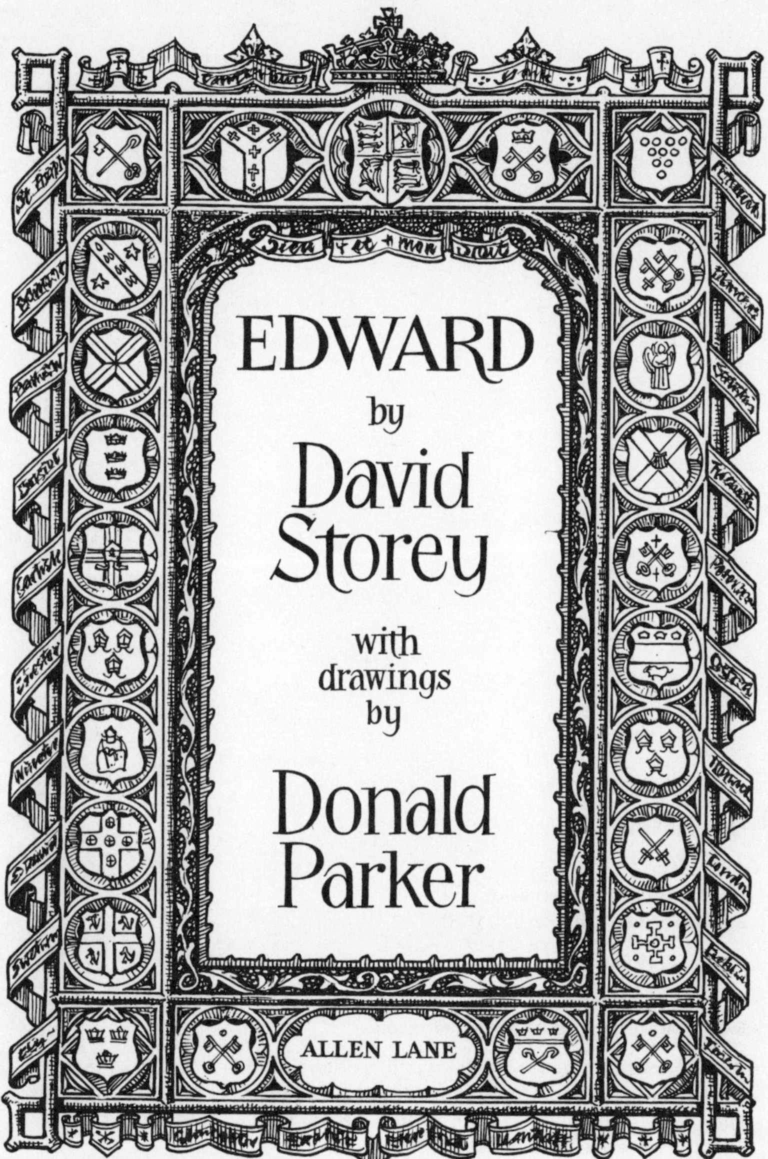

EDWARD

by

David Storey

with drawings by

Donald Parker

ALLEN LANE

First published in Great Britain in 1973

Allen Lane
A Division of Penguin Books Ltd
21 John Street, London WC1N 2BT

ISBN 0 7139 0680 4

Printed in Great Britain by
BAS Printers Limited, Wallop, Hampshire

Versions of seven of the drawings in this book first appeared in the *New Statesman*; one appeared in *The Teacher*; and one was used as publicity for the film and book *Heavens Above* in 1963.

Edward

Once upon a

there was a bishop.....

His name was Edward.

He was a man who liked to be prepared for all eventualities.....

come...........

what........

may.

He took an interest in many things.......

visited parishioners......

befriended the meek.....

believed in justice....

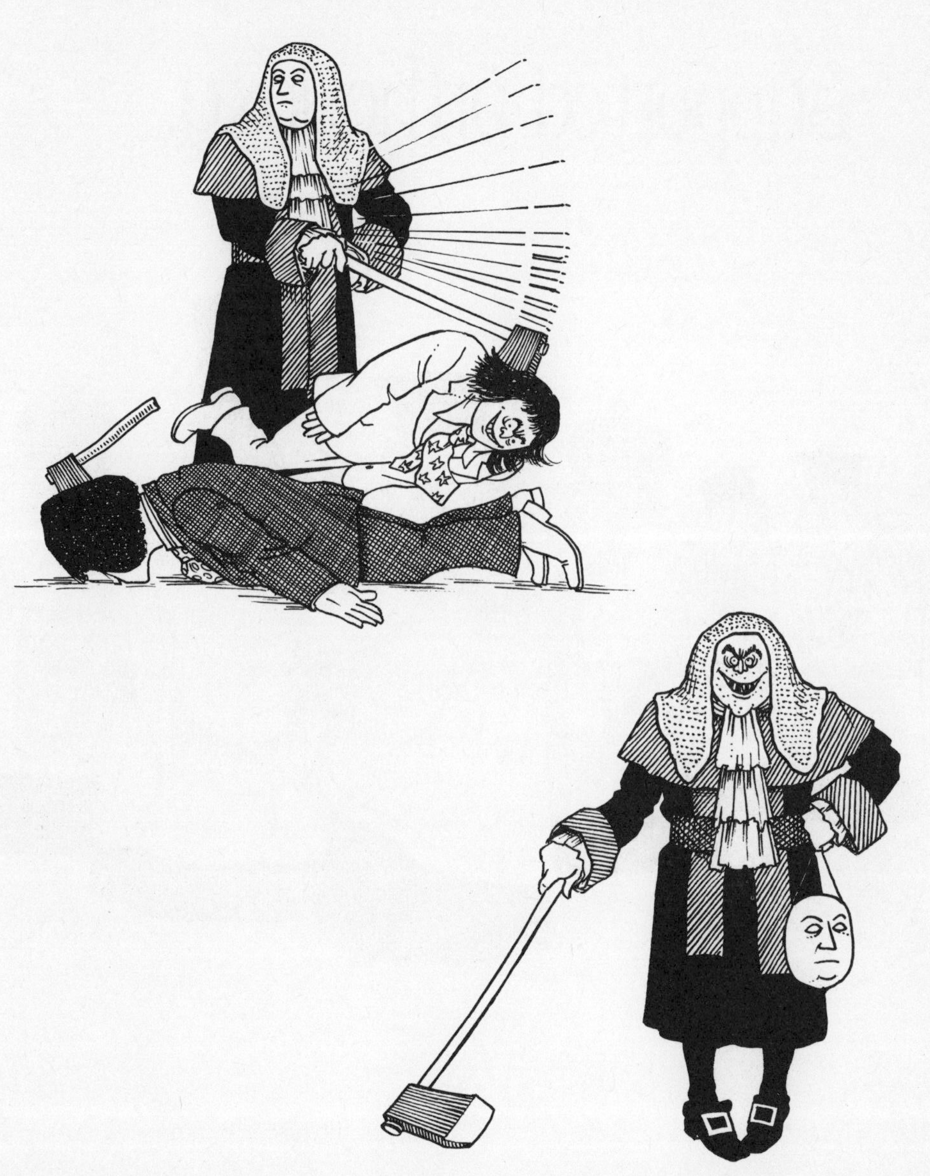

supported orthodoxy,

had no unusual habits

possessed a ready response.........

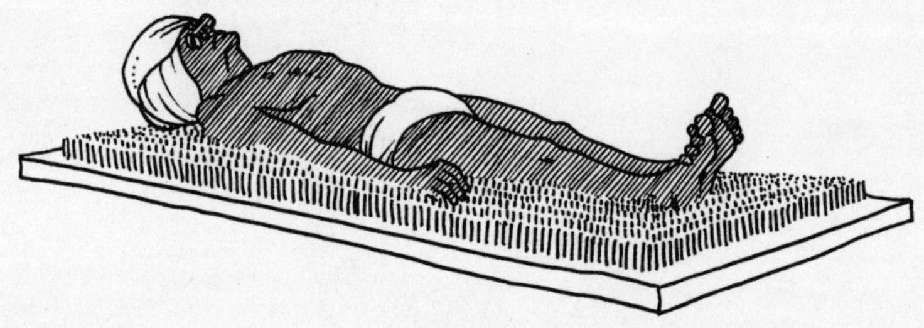

B

for the Devil's intrigues,

and looked for no
rewards, other than
those bestowed by
the One above.

He lived in a rural parish;

his house, though called a palace, was one of the traditional kind.

His wife was slightly
shorter than himself...

they had three sons

and had decided, in view
of the world's increasing
population......
they would have no more.

NOLI
ME
TANGERE

They cultivated pets...

people in need of care.....

& those who, in Edward's estimation, had lost the capacity for looking after themselves.

They had had,
on the whole,
a happy life......

had suffered the occasional vicissitude……

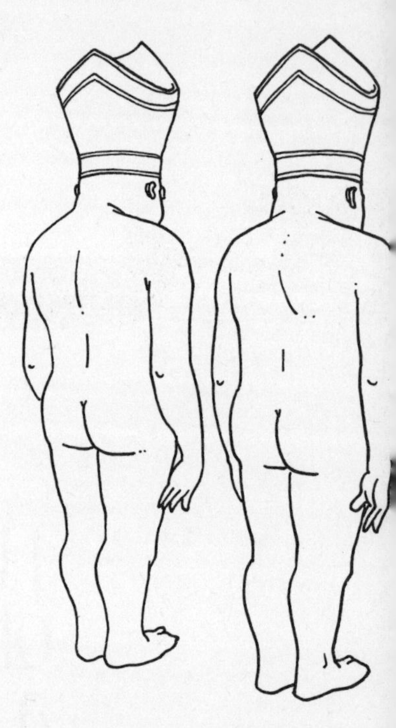

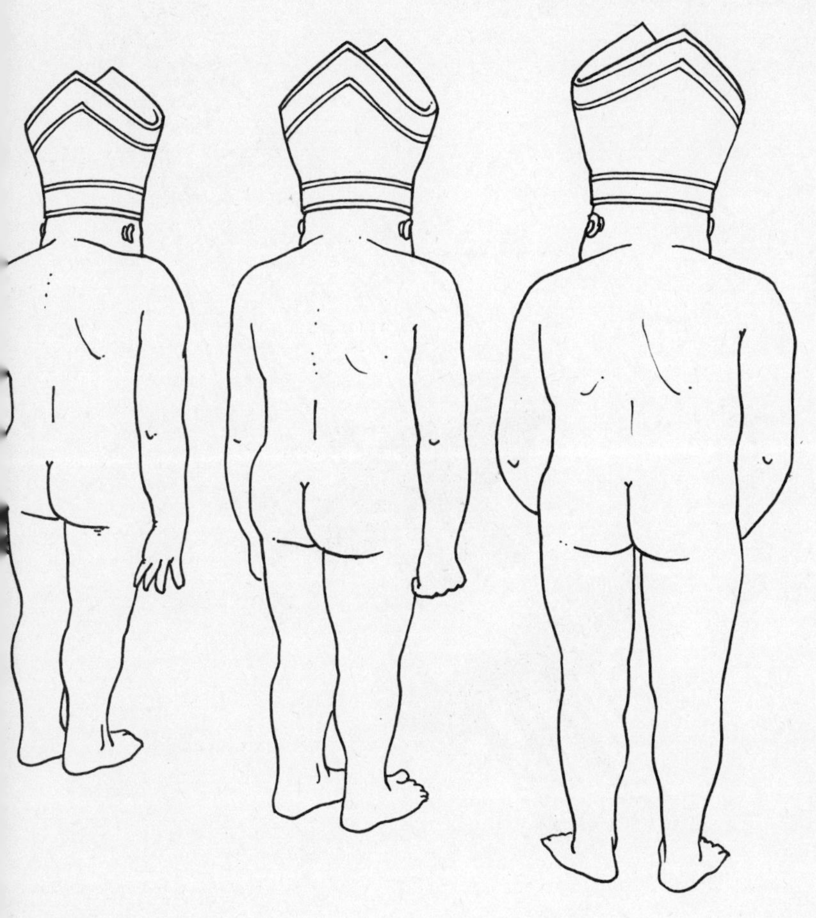

but, having endured, enjoyed a sense of well-being.......

at odd moments,
premonitions,

even.........

of salvation.

Edward was in his sixtieth year......

though on occasion,
of course,
he looked much younger....

and remarked to himself
from time to time as he
examined his face in
the morning mirror,
that he had lived, almost,
twice the life-span of
the Saviour Himself.

One day, engaged upon the composition of a sermon.......

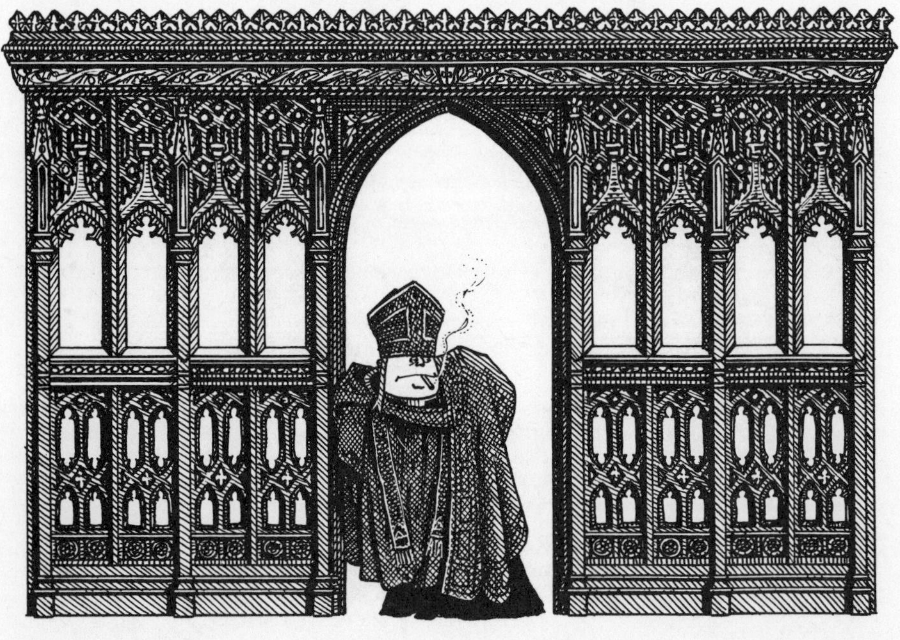

his happy brood
disporting themselves
on the lawn outside,

he happened to catch his finger in one of the many pieces of apparatus which, over a period of time, had accumulated on his desk,

and was shaking his finger
in irritation
when his
eye......

fell upon an object,
which, as far as he was
aware, it had never
fallen on before.

C

It was a small,
rectangular,
plain,
wooden,
lightly-varnished
box.

Inside, when he opened it, lay a metal key.

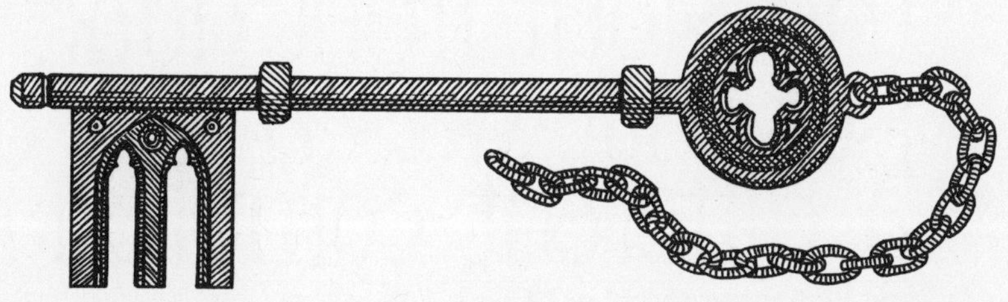

It was a large key; at least, it was larger than those keys normally in use about the official residence –

-save, that is, for the key used to unlock the stout front door. But that was a key of a different complexion altogether.....

He held it up...... he examined it from every angle.

He tried to imagine the circumstance in which a key of this nature - plainly of ecclesiastical origin - had come, with its plain wooden box, to be lying on his desk.

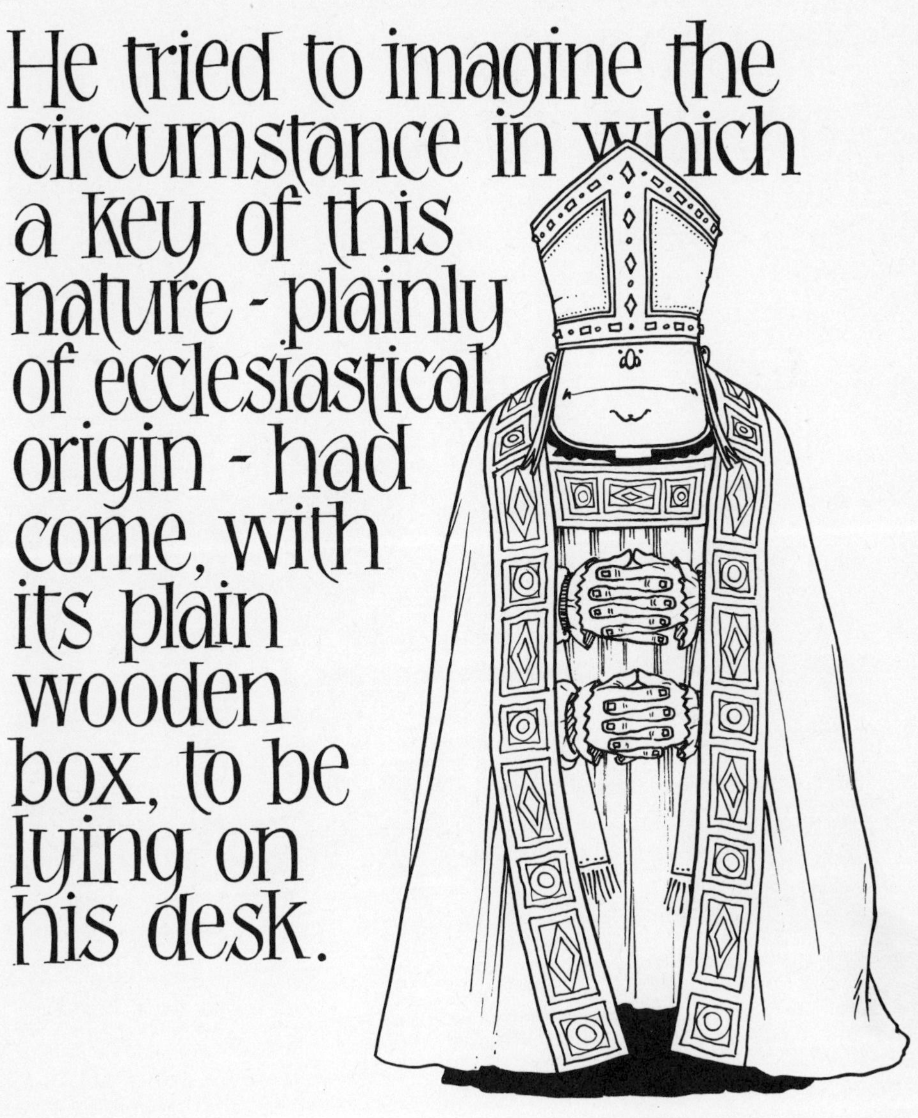

He tried it, tentatively, in the locks around him:

they, plainly, were
far too small:

the key itself was far too large.

He tried it, after a while,
in the door itself: he
tried it in every door he
came across; he enquired
of his wife, of his
children, of his secretary,
of his chaplain, of his
curates and vicars and
rectors and deacons;
he enquired of everyone
with whom he came
into contact -

casually, not overtly,
usually at the tail-end
of a conversation,

an interjection,
perfunctory, careless,
inconsequential,
in the midst of some more
mundane
appeal......

No one, it seemed, had ever seen it.........

neither wife,

nor child,

nor chaplain,

nor deacon......

He took it away with him on visits........
He took it on his annual holiday.

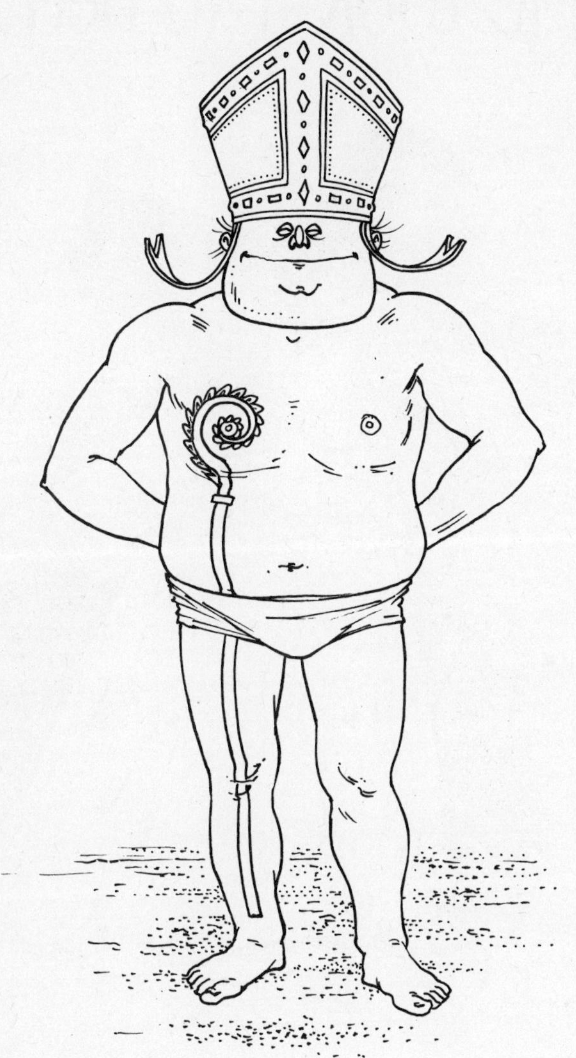

He took it to bed,

he took it to church,

it went in his car,

ED 1

it sat on his lap.
It became a memento....
and late at night, the
key laid out in the box
beside him, he would
muse on the lock into
which it might fit......
a door or a cupboard,
a safe or a chest.

A vision of riches
tormented his rest.

He was not, being
a bishop,
addicted to wealth.

He had a large mansion;
he had a fine car: he had
servants in church,
and servants without:
a chapel to pray in, a
cathedral to preach in;
a Father and Son to
grant his requests.

Perhaps - he imagined - the key guarded a secret:

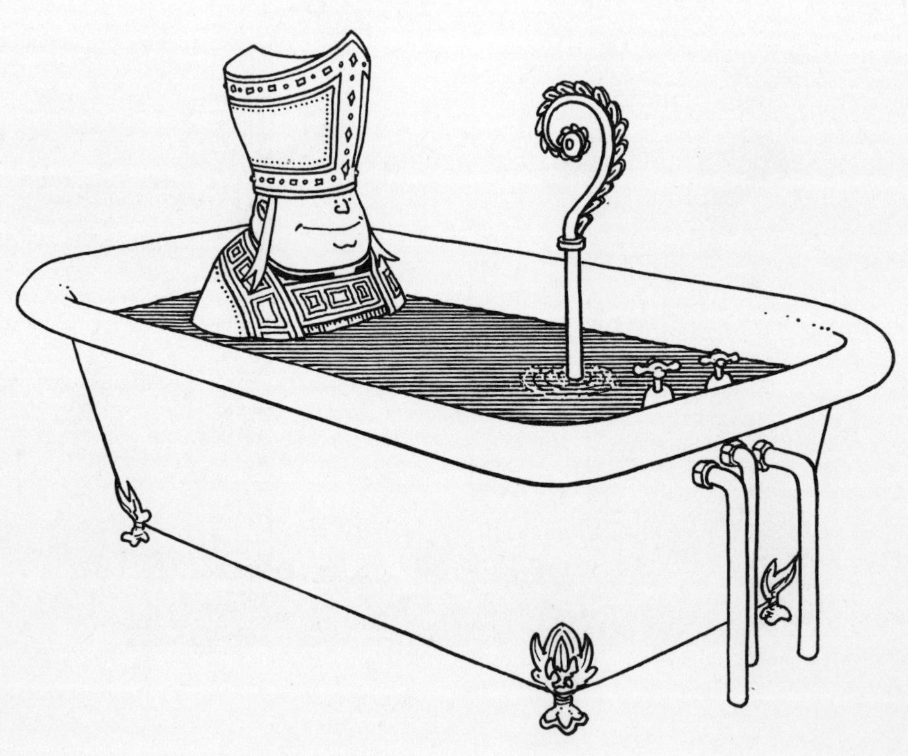

a prisoner;
a virgin;
a martyr,

D

a saint......

or guarded,
conceivably,
a chalice,
a relic......

or the Grail
of legendary fame
itself.

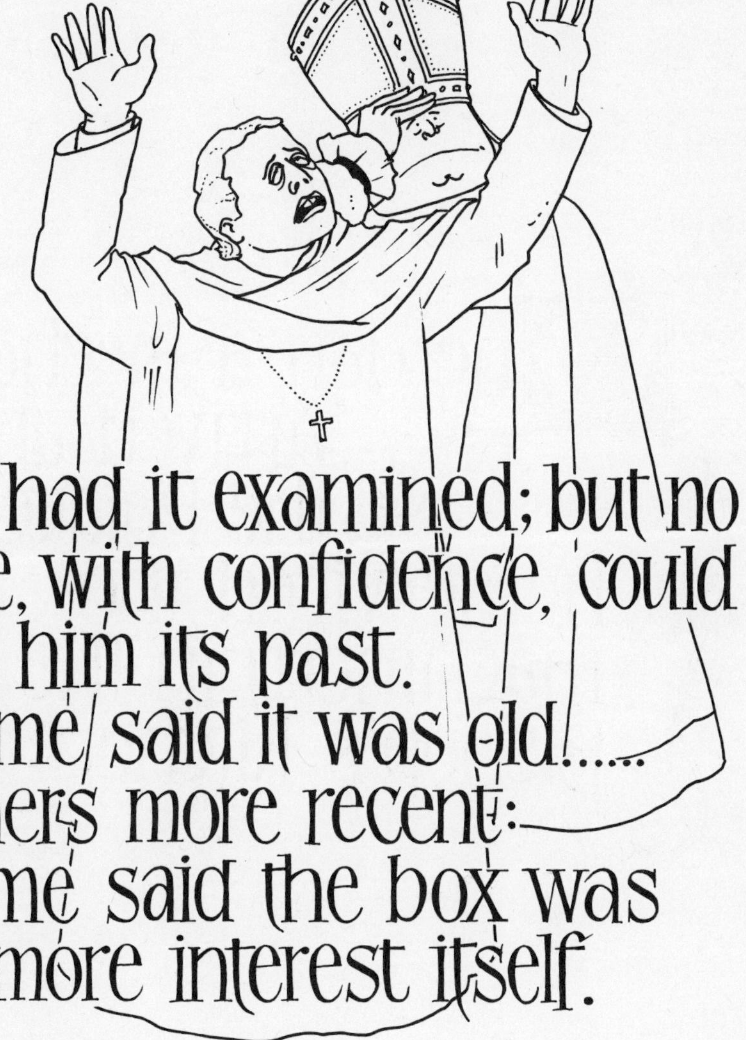

He had it examined; but no one, with confidence, could tell him its past.
Some said it was old......
others more recent:
some said the box was of more interest itself.

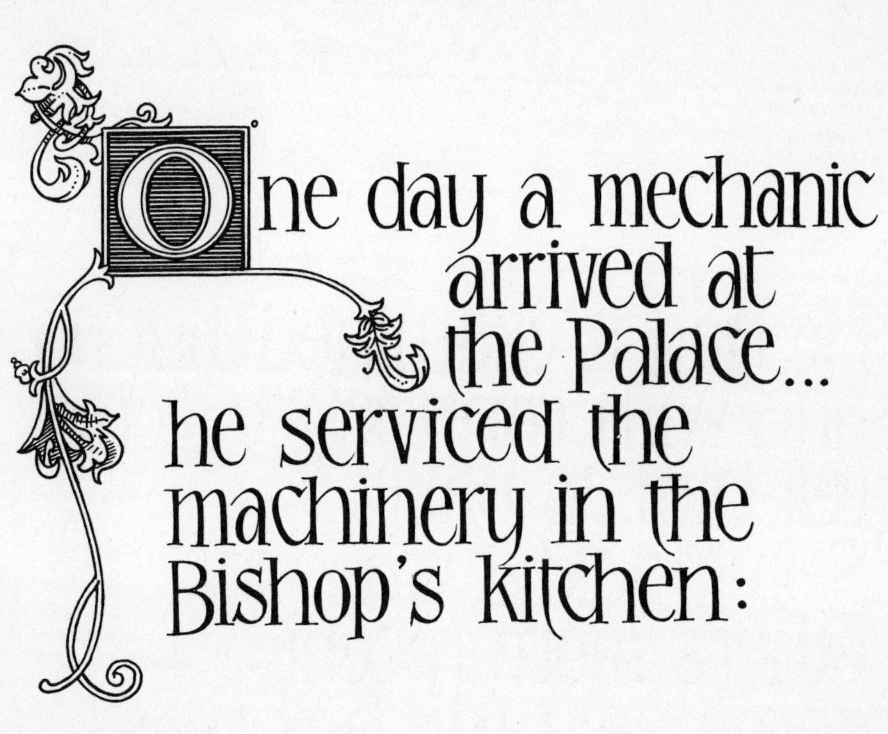

One day a mechanic arrived at the Palace...
he serviced the machinery in the Bishop's kitchen:

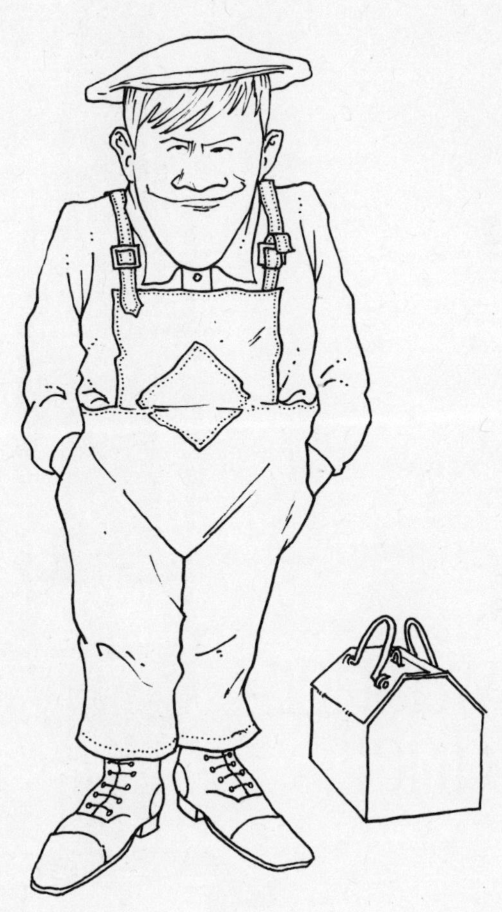

the washer,
the drier,

he examined the plugs.

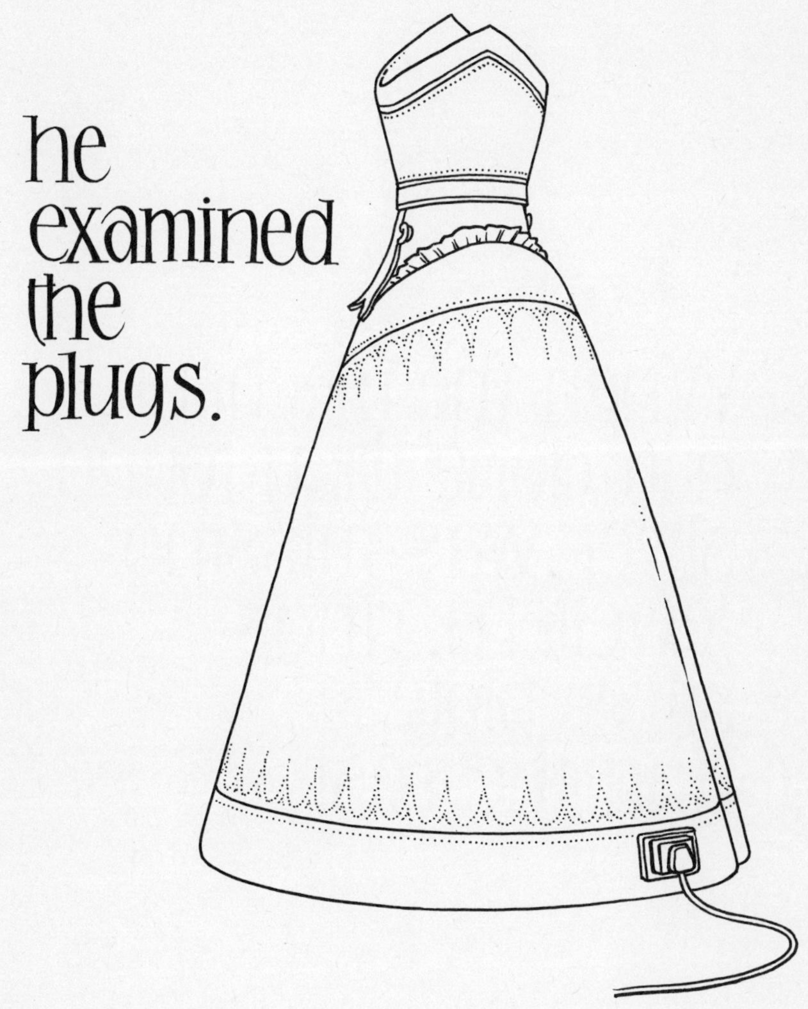

When the mechanic
had gone they found
silver was missing:
jewellery, rings,
silver plate
and the rest.

ihs

The mechanic, a day later, was found at the seaside.....
He was brought back to the palace,

and put under arrest.

Edward felt sorry for the mechanic himself...

He gave him a job when
he came out of prison: he
serviced not only his
palace but his churches;
repaired all the wiring,
maintained all the lamps;
polished the plate and
the cross and the chalice;
stoked up the boilers,
painted the woodwork,
ran up the flags and
tolled all the bells.

One day the mechanic
noticed the key on the
study desk.....
'Alas,' said the Bishop,
'I've had it some time,
but I can't find the
lock.'
'I'll make one for you,
your Grace,' the
mechanic told him,

and.......

in a few days
he put one together

so that

to this day

the Bishop......
with his wife and three children, his chapel, his house, his church and his pets, his provost, his car, his vicars and curates.......

has a lock he can
open

As easily and as quickly as he can open the rest.